First printing 2023

ISBN: 978-1-7398622-1-3

Wickham Publishing

wickhampublishing@yahoo.com

Some images contain mugs which are manufactured by Emma Bridgewater. These images are shared with permission.

Thank you to my family... my daughters, mum, sister and dad for your endless love, support and encouragement especially with the making of this book. What was a dream has become a reality and I couldn't have done it without you ... thank you … thank you for always being by my side.

xxx

And thank you to Ian and Georgia for taking on the publishing role, putting it all together and for making it real .. thank you.

I have always enjoyed looking at things like the clouds, rocks or my coffee and seeing what I can see in them ... it's now become a bit of a running joke... "here she goes again".

Being a keen photographer too, I started taking photographs of my coffee and the first photograph in this book was actually taken on the anniversary of my grandmother's death, at the time I wondered if it was her waving to us.

Since then, I have built up a collection of coffee images which I would like to share with you…

A lady waving.

A man wearing a cap, carrying a
huge rock and a pickaxe.

A brain.

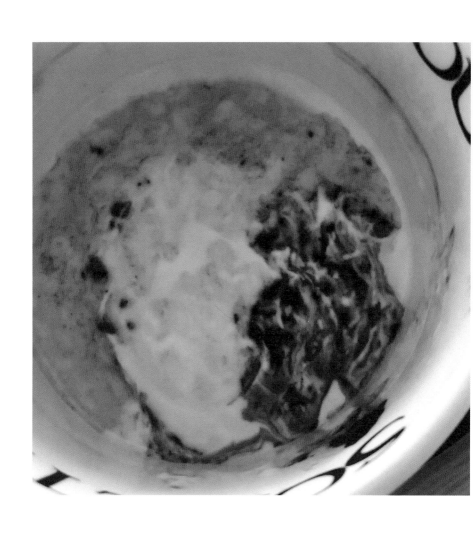

A large furry dog, like a
labradoodle.

8

A snail off on its travels.

A fetus.

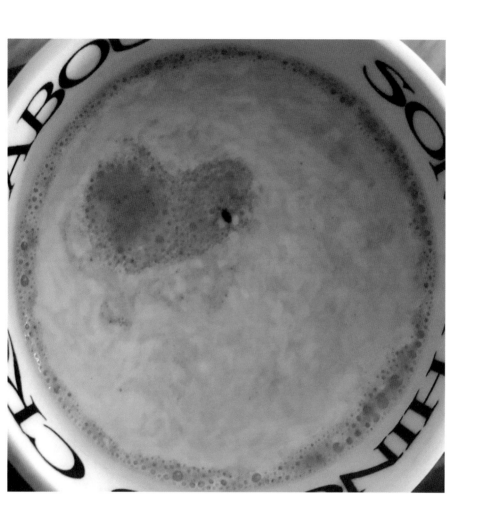

A love heart.

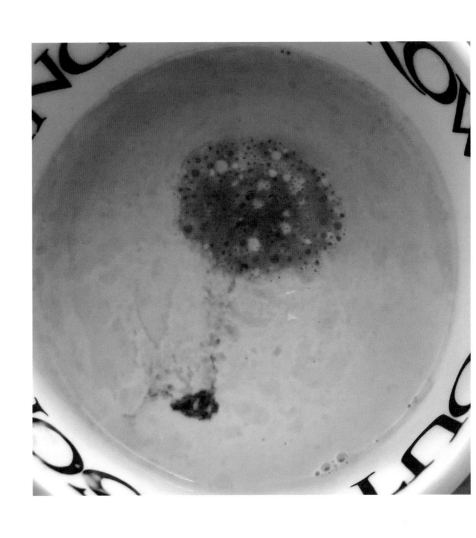

A balloon floating away.

A kangaroo holding her arm up.

A walking heart.

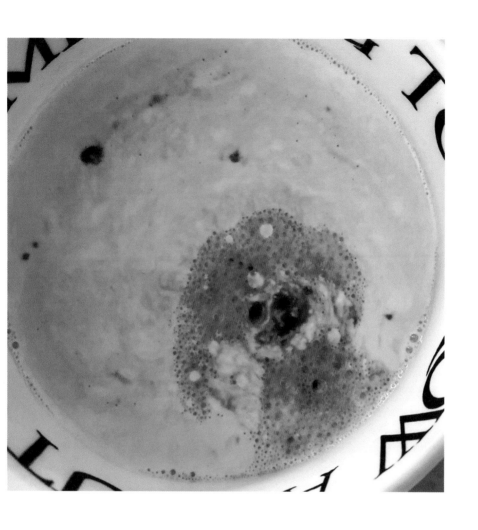

A smiley dog.

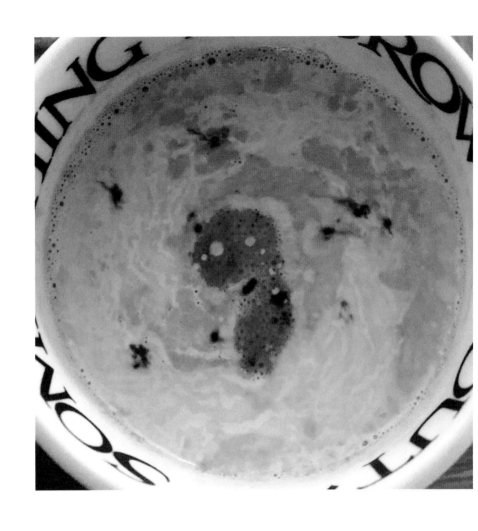

A little creature sitting.

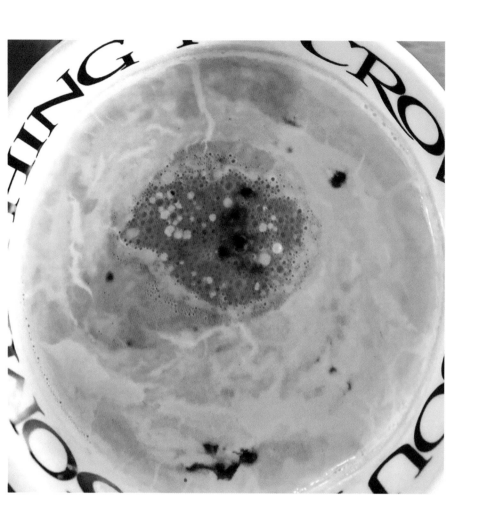

A garden bird.

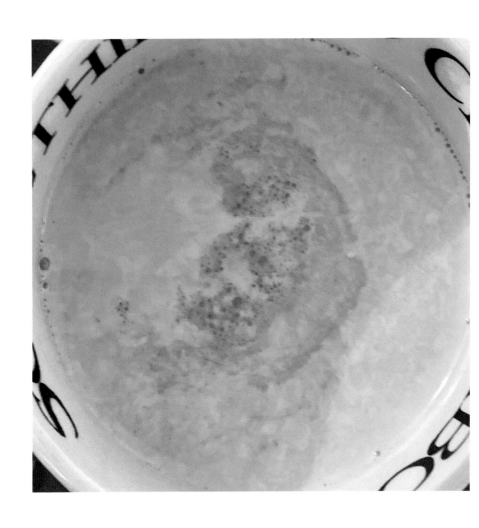

A mummy holding her baby.

A laughing moon.

A turkey off on a gander.

A sleeping moon.

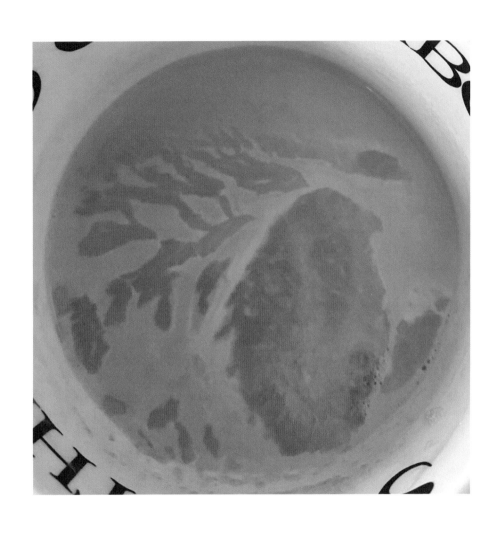

A buzzard in a tree.

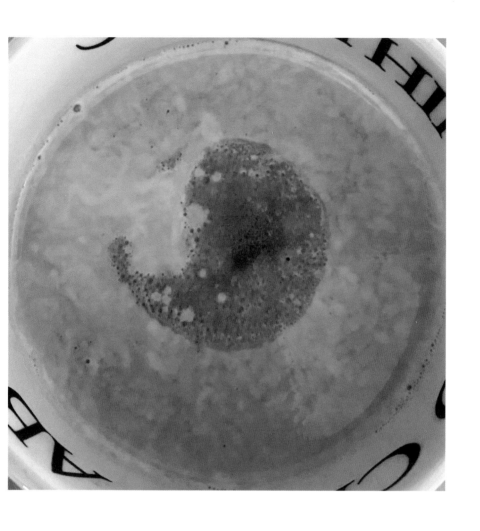

A moles face.

A sad face.

A fossil like mine.

An angel with a halo.

26

A surprised face.

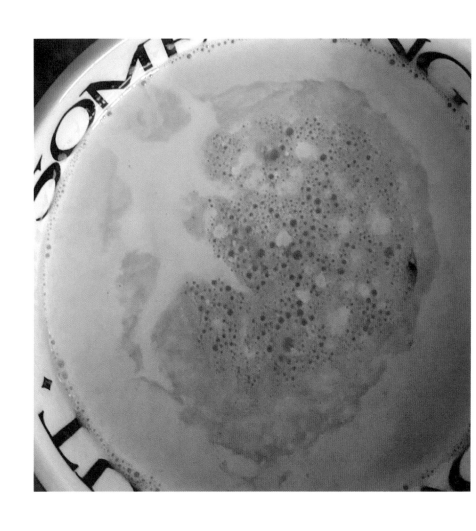

A person hiking with a backpack
on.

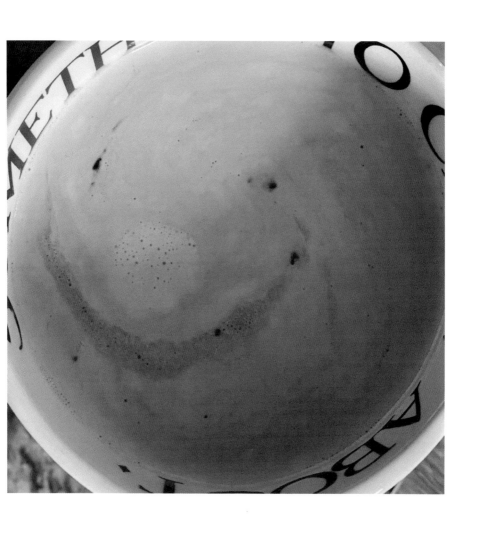

A smiley face.

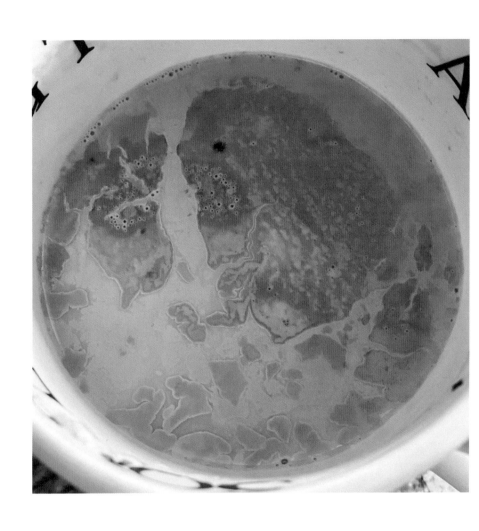

A baby bird.

A heart and head surrounded by
veins.

A dog off on a walk.

A stick man.

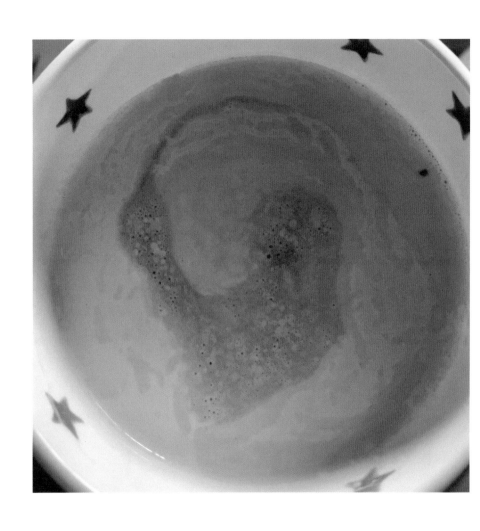

A ghost flying around.

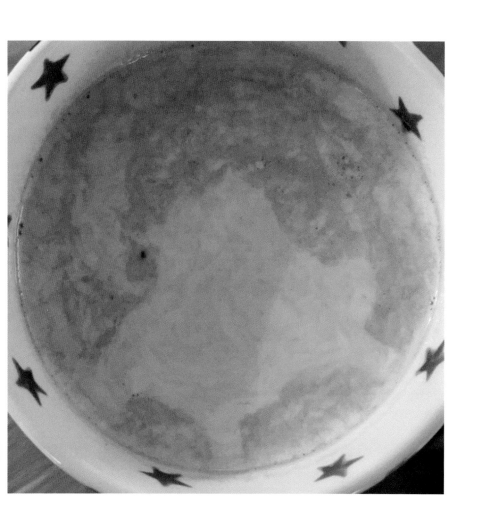

A turtle walking away.

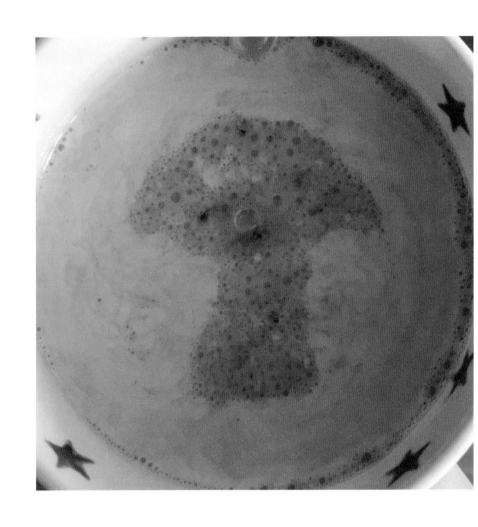

A mushroom.

A tree growing.

A froglet.

An elephant with no trunk.

A cat walking off with its tail
held high.

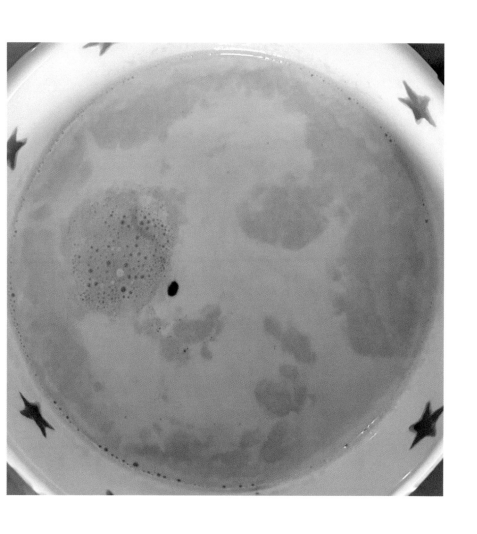

A poodle with a long face.

A penguin.

A heart.

A lady holding her arms out to
catch the child.

A giraffe, reminded me of the
film Madagascar.

An octopus.

A man waving a fire baton.

A dog with one ear sticking up.

48

An alien.

A pixie off collecting.

A person.

Angel wings.

A bug.

A rabbit with wings.

A dog's face.

A dragonfly.

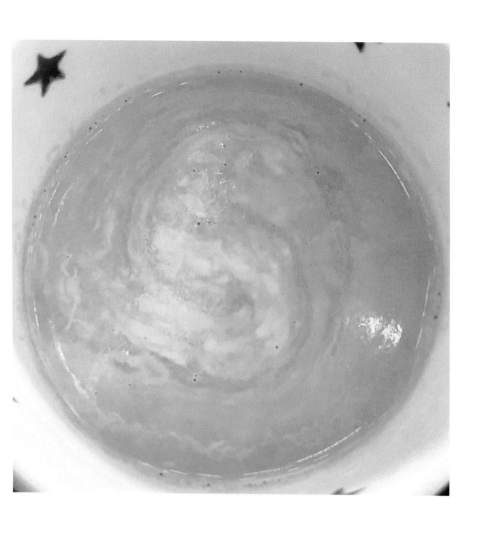

The letter 'S' or a snake.

Owls sitting together.

A dogs face looking back at us.

A Welsh dragon.

A goat.

A badgers face.

A wolf snarling.

A lone branch bending.

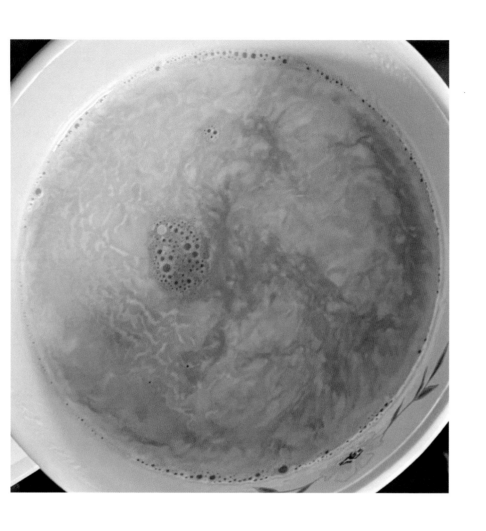

A dinosaur bird holding an egg.

A great danes head.

A crow sitting.

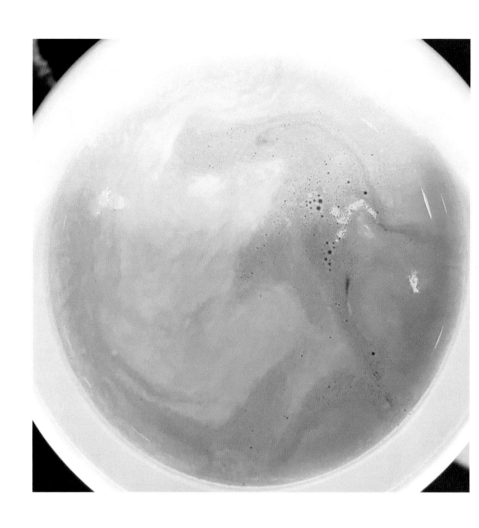

The Grinch's head.

A squirrel.

A turtle chasing food.

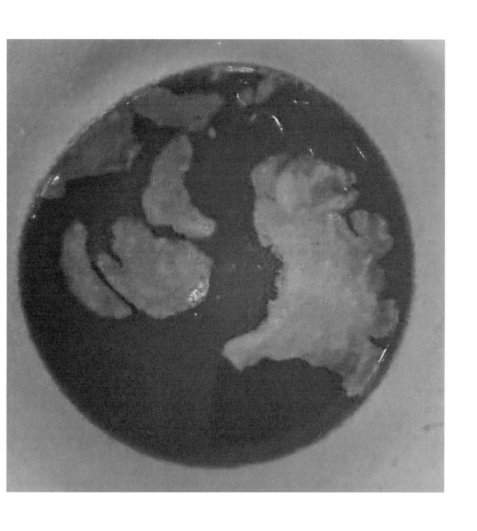

A dinosaur walking away.

A hedgehog.

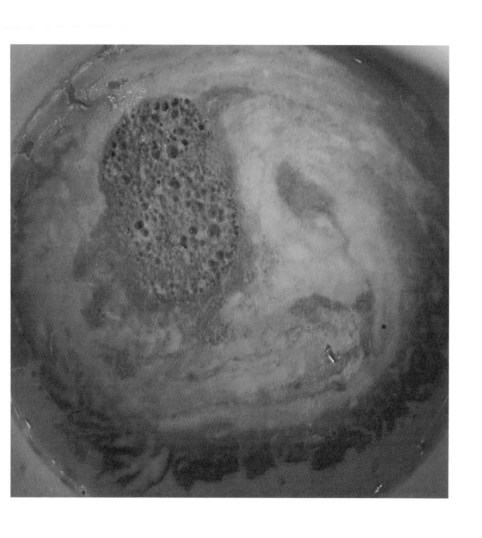

A penguin off on a walk.

A goldfish.

A firework.

A puffin.

A mountain.

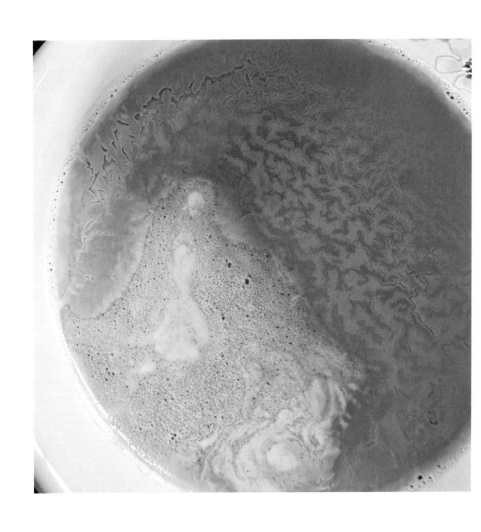

A lady walking.

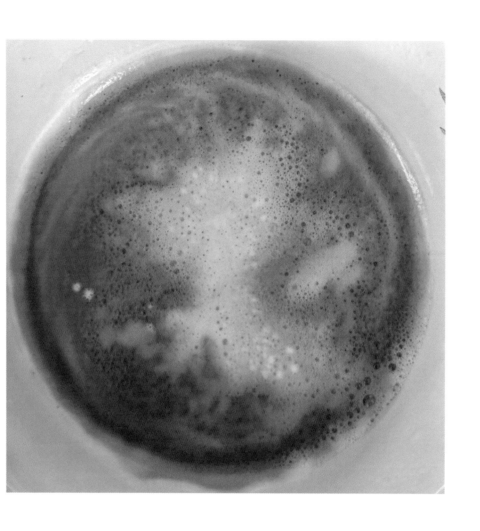

A baby dragon.

A large bear looking away.

A butterfly in the midst of chaos.

I hope you have enjoyed looking ...
What did you see?

Hannah sage was born in 1980 and grew up in Herefordshire which is where she lives today with her two daughters and their two dogs and four cats. By day Hannah is a registered childminder and in her spare time she enjoys nothing more than exploring with a camera in her hand!

Follow her journey on Instagram and share your findings.

@WHAT_DO_YOU_SEE_BY_HANNAH_SAGE

Printed in Poland
by Amazon Fulfillment
Poland Sp. z o.o., Wrocław
18 May 2023

0f9921f1-11b3-41cb-bca2-b49b8b873079R02